Bismillahir Rahmanir Rahim

This book belongs to:

ooooooooooooooooooooooooooooooooooooooooo

Illustrated by Gurmeet
First published 2012
© Goodword Books 2012

Goodword Books
1, Nizamuddin West Market
New Delhi-110 013
Tel. 9111-4182-7083, 4652-1511
Fax: 9111-4565-1771
email: info@goodwordbooks.com
www.goodwordbooks.com

Islamic Vision Ltd.
434 Coventry Road, Small Heath
Birmingham B10 0UG, U.K.
Tel. 121-773-0137
Fax: 121-766-8577
e-mail: info@ipci-iv.co.uk
www.islamicvision.co.uk

IB Publisher Inc.
81 Bloomingdale Rd, Hicksville
NY 11801, USA
Tel. 516-933-1000
Fax: 516-933-1200
Toll Free: 1-888-560-3222
email: info@ibpublisher.com
www.ibpublisher.com

Printed in India at Thomson Press

THE GREAT CALIPHS

Sr. Nafees Khan
Vinni Rehman
Maria Khan

Goodword

Contents

Abu Bakr Siddiq

(May Allah be pleased with him)

The First Caliph of Islam
573 C.E. - 634 C.E.

The Birth of Abu Bakr

Abu Bakr was born in 573 C.E., in the city of Makkah. His parents were Uthman bin Abu Qahafah and Ummul Khair. This noble and wealthy family belonged to the tribe of Quraysh, the same tribe as that of Muhammad ﷺ.

At birth he was named Abdul Kabah (servant of Kabah), and when he accepted Islam, he was named Abdullah (servant of Allah). However, he became known as Abu Bakr, the father of the camel, as he loved camels and knew a lot about them.

Abu Bakr was three years younger than the Prophet Muhammad ﷺ and, as they were very much alike, he became his childhood friend. Abu Bakr remained his closest Companion and the Prophet once said, 'No one has been a better companion to me than Abu Bakr.'

Abu Bakr: The Man

When Prophet Muhammad ﷺ was twelve years old, he had gone to Syria with his uncle, Abu Talib, with a trading caravan. During that trip, Bahira (a monk) on seeing Muhammad ﷺ predicted that one day he would be a prophet. Abu Bakr was also with the caravan. From that day onwards, Abu Bakr was convinced that this prophecy would come true.

Abu Bakr was known for his good character. He was honest and truthful; hardworking and fair in his dealings. He was extremely kind and helped the poor and the sick. He spoke eloquently and enjoyed composing poetry. He was intelligent and had an excellent memory.

As a merchant he traveled a lot and the experiences he had on his journeys broadened his general knowledge and outlook on life.

Asma and Abdullah were born to Abu Bakr's first wife, Qutaila. Abdur Rahman and Ayisha were born to Umm Ruman his second wife. Muhammad ibn Abu Bakr was born to his third wife, Asma. Umm Kulsoom was born after his death to his fourth wife, Habibah.

Abu Bakr Accepts Islam

In 610 C.E., Prophet Muhammad ﷺ was told by Angel Jibrail that he has been chosen as the messenger of Allah. Three family members, Khadija, 'Ali and Zaid bin Harith (the Prophet's adopted son) immediately accepted Islam. Abu Bakr was the first person outside the family to do so without any hesitation.

Abu Bakr was a rich merchant. He knew that his acceptance of Islam would have a negative affect on his business. However, he made up his mind to support Islam at any cost.

He made no secret of his conversion to Islam. He

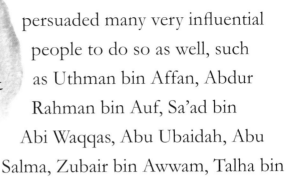

persuaded many very influential
people to do so as well, such
as Uthman bin Affan, Abdur
Rahman bin Auf, Sa'ad bin
Abi Waqqas, Abu Ubaidah, Abu
Salma, Zubair bin Awwam, Talha bin
Ubaidullah and several others. All these
men were of a high status and proved to
be a great asset to Islam.

Al-Siddiq

Slaves who accepted Islam were
persecuted and tortured by their owners.

Abu Bakr purchased many of them and set
them free. Bilal, the first *muadhdhin* (the
one who calls for prayer) of Islam was
one of them.

Wherever Muhammad ﷺ went, Abu
Bakr went with him and he

often risked his life to protect the Prophet.

After the death of his wife Khadija and his uncle Abu Talib, the Holy Prophet was sad. Things were not going well for Muslims either. One night in 620 C.E. the Prophet was taken to the Heavens (*al-Mi'raj*). People ridiculed him when they heard that he had gone to al-Masjid al-Aqsa in Jerusalem and from there to the Heavens.

A number of people, some of them Muslims, came to Abu Bakr and expressed doubts about the possibility of this journey. He silenced them with his eloquent reasoning and told them that he would believe anything the Prophet said. Thus he earned the title of *'al-Siddiq'* which means a very strong and honest friend.

A Little Intolerance

A man came up and insulted Abu Bakr one day when he was sitting with the Prophet. Abu Bakr listened but remained silent. The man insulted him again. But Abu Bakr continued to hold his peace. When the man kept on with his verbal attack, Abu Bakr could no longer control himself, and answered back. On hearing this, the Prophet immediately got up to leave... 'Why have you left your place, Prophet of God?' Abu Bakr asked. 'As long as you remained silent, Abu Bakr,' the Prophet replied, 'God's angel was answering for you. But as soon as you burst out, the angel left, and I am leaving too.'

BYZANTINE

BLACK SEA

GREECE

CRETE

CYPRUS

MEDITERREAN SEA

EGYPT

The Surah Ar-Rum

Four years later a war broke out between
the Persians and the Byzantines. The
Quraish sympathized with the Persians and
the Muslims with the Byzantines, who were
Christians.

PERSIA

PERSIAN GULF

ARABIA

The *Surah ar-Rum* was revealed at this stage. It predicted that a day would come when the Christians would win (30:4). Even some of the Muslims had doubts about this, because the Persians were powerful at that time. But Abu Bakr was sure that the prophecy would come true.

Ubaiy bin Khalf, a Quraish leader, made a bet with Abu Bakr that the Persians would win. They agreed that the loser would pay one hundred camels. This agreement was binding on their heirs as well. Nine years later, the prophecy came true. The

heirs of Ubaiy not only honored this agreement but accepted Islam as well, because they saw the truth in it. Abu Bakr gave away all the camels as *sadaqa* (charity).

In the Cave of Thawr

When the persecution in 622 C.E. became intolerable, the Muslims started migrating in batches to Yathrib (Madinah).

Allah revealed to the Prophet Muhammad ﷺ that the Quraish were plotting to kill him. One night under the cover

of darkness, he left Makkah accompanied by Abu Bakr and a guide. They took an indirect and longer route because they knew the Makkans would be searching for them along the direct route to Madinah. They stayed in the Cave of Thawr for three days and nights. Asma, Abu Bakr's daughter, brought them food in the dead of night.

When the Quraish learned of this, they were very upset and offered a reward of one hundred camels to whosoever brought the Prophet back to Makkah. One search party followed close on the heels of the Prophet, but when they reached the mountain, they lost trace of him. They then

climbed the mountain, and passed by the cave in which he and Abu Bakr were hiding. Noting a spider's web on the mouth of the cave, they said to one another, 'If he had entered this cave, the spider's web would not have remained intact.'

The First Mosque

When Prophet Muhammad ﷺ and Abu Bakr reached Quba, on the outskirts of Madinah, they

built a mosque there. When they reached Madinah, they received a very warm and grand welcome. The first thing the Prophet wanted to do was to build a mosque there as well. Abu Bakr paid for the land where it was to be built. Both of them participated in the construction of this mosque, now known as al-Masjid al-Nabawi.

To help settle the newcomers, Prophet Muhammad ﷺ paired each one of them with a person from Madinah, thus establishing a 'brotherhood'.

Prophet Muhammad ﷺ consulted Abu Bakr in all important matters and his advice was often accepted. The Prophet used to say that Abu Bakr was the best counselor. During meetings Abu Bakr often sat on the right side of the Prophet.

After being in Madinah for some time, Abu Bakr's daughter Ayishah was married to Prophet Muhammad ﷺ, which brought Abu Bakr and the Prophet even closer.

The Tabuk Expedition

In order to finance the Tabuk expedition (630 C.E.) on the Syrian border, the Prophet invited the Muslims to contribute towards it. Uthman gave ten thousand camels and Umar contributed half of his wealth. When Abu Bakr came with his contributions, the Prophet asked as to what he had left behind for himself and

his family. Abu Bakr said, "I have brought all that I had. I have Allah and His Prophet left for myself and my family!"

First Amirul Hajj

In 631, three hundred Muslims were sent to perform Hajj by the Prophet under the leadership of Abu Bakr. He thus became the first Amir ul Hajj (leader of the pilgrimage) in the history of Islam.

A short time after performing his '*Hajjatul Wada*'' (the Farewell pilgrimage) in 632 C.E., the Prophet fell sick and appointed Abu Bakr to lead the prayers (*salat*). Ayishah felt that her father, a kind-hearted person, would become emotional and would not be able to do so. The Prophet insisted that Abu Bakr alone was

the most suitable person to lead the prayers. Thus, during the lifetime of the Prophet, Abu Bakr was given the highest office in Islam.

Soon after this the Prophet passed away. Everyone was grief-stricken. 'Umar was so upset that he said he would kill anyone who said that the Prophet had died.

At this crucial moment Abu Bakr used his eloquence to calm the people, "Listen to me, O people. Those of you who worshipped Muhammad ﷺ know that he is dead like any other mortal. But those of you who worship Allah know that He is alive and will live forever." Then he quoted some verses of the Quran. This indeed had a calming effect on the people.

The First Caliph

This was a great emergency and a new leader had to be elected. Arguments started amongst the Ansars (the People of the Madinah) and the Muhajirs (those who migrated to Madinah from Makkah) as to who should be the Caliph. Before the situation became serious, both 'Umar and Abu Ubaidah said to Abu Bakr, "O Siddiq, you are the best amongst the Muslims. You were the 'Second of the two' in the

Cave (9:40).You were appointed as Amir ul Hajj. The Prophet appointed you to lead the prayers during his illness. Of all the Companions you were the closest and the dearest to the Prophet. Hold out your hand so that we may pledge loyalty to you!"

After that, everyone present agreed to this suggestion and took an oath of loyalty. Abu Bakr gave a speech asking the people to support him, saying, "…..you must obey me as long as I obey Allah and His Messenger. If I disobey Allah and His Messenger, you are free to disobey me!" He also added, '……..if people give up striving for the cause of Allah, Allah sends down disgrace on them. If people become evil-doers, Allah sends down calamities on them.'

The Syrian Expedition

A few weeks before the Prophet's death, preparations were being made to lead an expedition to Syria (632 C.E.) under the leadership of Usama ibn Zayd. After his death

many people were against this as Abu Bakr and the Muslims were facing many problems. The country was almost on the verge of civil war and the troops were needed at home for the defense of Madinah.

There were tribes whose faith was not strong and were rebelling to the point of leaving Islam. People thought that the death of the Prophet would put an end to Islam. Many did not want to pay the *zakat*. There were a number of imposters who claimed to be the next prophet.

Abu Bakr put his trust in Allah and remained firm in his faith. His unshakeable faith proved that Islam was a way of life. He was determined to

protect all the basic beliefs of Islam. Also, he refused to call back the expedition to Syria, saying, 'Come what may, I am not going to call it back as it was ordered to go by the Prophet himself.'

The Code of Conduct for War

Abu Bakr sent Usama ibn Zayd off to Syria with the following code of conduct for war, which remains a model to this day:

'Be truthful. Do not deceive anyone. Be kind to the men under you. Do not mutilate anyone. Do not kill the aged, women and children. Do not set fire to date palms or cut down fruit trees. Do not slaughter animals except for food. You will find monks in the monasteries. Leave them alone! Be respectful to the leaders of the enemy. Always fear Allah.'

Usama Bin Zayd was successful in his mission and returned after forty days, proving that Islam was there to stay. Upon Usama's return, Abu Bakr himself marched against the rebellious tribes. Within a few months all the revolts had been put down.

Khalid ibn al-Walid, the greatest young general of Islam, played a major role in this. His strategies and courage brought astonishing results within two years. He was not only able to make Arabia safe for Islam but he was successful in expanding its borders as well.

The Compilation of the Quran

In 633 C.E Musaylimah, a self-proclaimed prophet, was defeated in a fierce battle at Yamama. During this battle most of the Companions who had memorized the Quran were martyred. Umar was the first to feel the need for a written copy of the Quran. He feared that if the Quran was not written down, there was the chance that it would be altered or forgotten.

Initially, Abu Bakr was reluctant to take up the task. In the end he agreed to do so as Umar continued to press him with logical arguments.

Zayid bin Thabit, who was the Prophet's main scribe, was given this task. Zayid collected the text of the verses dictated by the Prophet and written down during his lifetime from whoever had them in their possession. Abu Bakr, Umar and other senior Companions, who were the *huffaz* (memorizers), checked for accuracy and made sure that strict guidelines were followed.

Umar: His Successor

At the age of sixty three (634 C.E.), Abu Bakr fell ill and realized that his end was coming near. Even during his illness, he was concerned about the future of Islam after his death. He did not want Muslims to face problems similar to the ones he had had after the death of the Prophet.

Abu Bakr had often consulted Umar and accepted his advice. He decided to put the nomination of Umar before the senior Companions saying, 'My brothers in faith, I have not appointed any of my own relatives as your Caliph. I have

appointed a man who is the fittest among you. Do you accept him?' Most of them accepted Abu Bakr's proposal.

The Death of Abu Bakr

Before his death, he told his family to bury him in the same sheet that he was wearing. The family was to sell his land and pay back to the public treasury the salary that he had received during the two years and three months that he had been the Caliph.

His funeral prayer was led by Umar and he was buried in Madinah next to his lifelong friend, his beloved Prophet. He was with the Prophet during his lifetime and now in death he is still by his side!!

Umar Farooq

(May Allah be pleased with him)

The Second Caliph of Islam
582 C.E. - 644 C.E.

Al-Farooq

The Prophet Muhammad ﷺ gave Umar the title of "Al Farooq", which means, 'The one who distinguishes between right and wrong.' Once the Prophet said, "Allah has placed truth

upon Umar's tongue and heart." He also said, "The truth after me is with Umar, wherever he may be."

These were the qualities which made Umar Farooq an extraordinary person. In the history of the world, he holds a unique position among the greatest of the kings, statesmen and administrators. Unlike them he was not guided by worldly ambition, but by his faith in Allah, His messenger and His book—the Quran. He became the head of the largest state in the world, but he himself lived the life of a common man, simple in his habits and austere in his living. Even the poorest person could reach him directly and he was concerned about all his citizens, whether they were Muslims or non-Muslims.

Umar was born in Makkah around 582 C.E. Both his father Khattab and his mother, Khantamah, were prominent members of the 'Adi, a branch of the Quraish, a clan from which judges and ambassadors were chosen. Whenever the Quraish had any disputes amongst themselves or with others, they were chosen as arbitrators. They were held in great respect as they could speak eloquently and possessed tact and judgment.

Umar: A Man of Conviction

As a young boy, like those of his age, Umar also had to graze camels, goats and sheep, but unlike other children of Makkah, he learned to read and write. As a matter of fact, there were only sixteen other people in the whole of Makkah who could do so. This was surely a great achievement.

Umar grew up to be tall, with a very strong physique and an impressive personality. He was a champion wrestler and swordsman and was so accomplished as a rider that he could ride the wildest of horses with ease.

Umar, sincere and straightforward, had strong convictions. He was extremely intelligent. He was always ready to help the weak. An amazing quality which Umar had was that he was always eager to learn from everyone. He was free from all kind of prejudices. He was interested in knowing his mistakes and to

correct them. He was always very grateful to those who pointed out his faults and disliked those who tried to flatter him.

He displayed all the ancestral qualities including the art of public speaking and knowledge of genealogy. He had no difficulty in handling the responsibilities of an ambassador or in acting as an arbitrator for the Quraish.

As a rich successful merchant, he traveled to many foreign lands such as Iraq, Syria, Persia and Yemen and met all kinds of people including Arabian and Persian princes. This experience

broadened his insight into the needs and problems and the nature of people.

The Surah Ta Ha

The Prophet Muhammad ﷺ received his first revelation in 610 C.E. Later on when he started preaching about Islam the Quraish got angry and upset. They started to torture the Muslims, and eventually after some years when it became unbearable Muslims chose to leave Makkah. Umar was about twenty-seven years of age at that time and, whenever someone accepted Islam, he would become furious. He believed that this new faith was sacrilege against their various gods. Being a young man with strong convictions, he took it upon himself to stop the spread of this new religion in every possible way.

One day in 616 C.E., Umar set out, sword in hand, to kill the Prophet. On the way, a friend of his informed him that his own sister, Fatima had accepted Islam. Umar couldn't believe it, and to know the truth he went straight to her house. Fatima was reading the twentieth *Surah, Ta Ha* of the Quran and he heard the recitation. Fatima quickly hid it when she realized that Umar was there. After some exchange of words, Umar started beating his brother-in-law, Sa'eed. When Fatima tried to intervene she too was struck, which caused her to bleed. Fatima declared, "Umar, you can do what you like, but you cannot turn us away from Islam!" Umar loved his sister dearly and was moved at the sight of her blood and by her determination to follow her new faith. Overwhelmed with regret and guilt, he asked his sister to show him what she was reading. She handed him over the *Surah Ta Ha,* and he started reading it.

When he reached verse 14, 'I am Allah. There is no deity save Me; so worship Me alone, and say your prayers in My remembrance', he felt as if these verses were addressed to him in person and Allah was talking to him. He immediately decided not to lose any more time in following the truth. He turned to his sister and brother-in-law and said, "I came to

you as an enemy of Islam; I go from you as a friend of Islam.
I buckled on this sword to slay the Prophet of Islam; I now go
to him to offer my allegiance." Fatima and Sa'eed called out,
"*Allahu Akbar*!" (God is great!) He went to the Prophet and
professed his faith in Islam. Soon everyone in Makkah came
to know that Umar was no longer a bitter
enemy of Islam but a staunch follower.
He was the fortieth person to become a
Muslim.

Prayer of the Prophet

The conversion of Umar to Islam was in response to the prayer which the Prophet Muhammad ﷺ had made in the Kabah, "O Lord, make Islam strong with the conversion of either of the two men, Amr bin Hisham or Umar bin Al Khattab!"

Until now the Muslims had kept their faith private and prayed in secret. Umar asked, " O Messenger of Allah, are we not on the truth?" The Prophet answered, "Yes, we are indeed on the truth!" Umar continued, "Then why do we pray in hiding? Isn't it the time for us to declare our faith openly?" Umar persisted with his request until the Prophet agreed. Eventually, the Prophet Muhammad ﷺ led the prayers publicly for the first time in the Kabah.

A Unique Brotherhood

By 622 C.E., the persecution of the Muslims had reached its peak, and they started migrating quietly in batches with the Prophet's permission. Umar left for Madinah accompanied by twenty others after announcing his intentions openly, but nobody among Quraish had the courage to stop him.

Upon his arrival in Madinah, the Prophet Muhammad ﷺ established a unique and strong 'brotherhood' to help settle the *'Muhajirs'* (migrants) with the *'Ansars'* (the people of Madinah). Utban bin Malik, who was a chieftain, was chosen as Umar's brother-in-faith.

Virtue, Knowledge and Faith

With the growth in the numbers of Muslims, the Prophet wanted to decide upon a way of calling the faithful to prayers. He and some *Sahaba* (Companions) started considering the use of some kind of musical instrument similar to that of the Jews and the Christians, but at that point, Umar related a dream he had had, and suggested, "Why not appoint a man for this purpose?" The Prophet then sent for Bilal and asked him to perform the '*adhan*' (the call to prayers). Therefore, the credit goes to Umar for the establishment of the '*adhan*', which is echoed in every mosque around the globe to this day. He was the one who also inserted the line 'Prayer is better than sleep' in the *adhan* for morning prayers.

Subsequently, it was he who instituted the prayers of Tarawih in congregation in the mosque in the month of Ramadan. It was he who established the Hijri calendar, which began in the year of hijrah (Migration).

From the time of Migration till the death of the Prophet, Umar was actively involved in all the important events. The Prophet consulted with Abu Bakr and Umar in all matters of significance. The Prophet Muhammad ﷺ once said, "If you two agreed upon any matter, I would not oppose you."

As Umar was generous, he was always eager to contribute financially to the cause of Islam and gave away most of his wealth for it. He stood by the side of the Prophet in all his trials and tribulations. His love for the Prophet knew no bounds. In 625 C.E, Hafsah, the widowed daughter of Umar was married to the Prophet Muhammad ﷺ, which further brought them closer.

On the Death of the Prophet

When the Prophet Muhammad ﷺ passed away in 632 C.E. after a brief illness, everyone was grief stricken. Umar was

beside himself with shock. He could not imagine how Islam and Muslims would cope without him. Abu Bakr, trying to calm the people said, "O people, those of you who worshipped Muhammad know that he is dead like any other mortal. But those who worship Allah know that He is alive and will live forever." But Umar was still inconsolable and then, Abu Bakr quoted the following verses of the Quran. "Muhammad is only a messenger. Messengers have passed away before him. If he should die, or be killed, will you turn back on your heels? Those who turn on their heels do not harm the Lord in the least. Allah will reward the grateful. No soul should die except with Allah's permission and at an appointed time." (3:144,145)

Later, recalling this day, Umar narrated, "By God, I heard Abu Bakr recite these verses. I was so

dumbfounded that my legs would not bear me, and I fell to the ground, knowing that the Holy Prophet was indeed dead."

The *Ansars* had gathered at a meeting place and were arguing as to who should be the leader, after Prophet's death. When Abu Bakr, Umar and Abu Ubaidah arrived there, they found the Muslim community was on the verge of splitting. Thinking quickly, Umar, took the initiative and declared his support for Abu Bakr by pointing out the various hints given by the Prophet Muhammad ﷺ on this subject.

Abu Bakr was a Caliph for only a short time and Umar was one of his chief advisors. It was Umar who had convinced Abu Bakr to have the Quran compiled in the form of a book after the battle of Yamama.

Leader of the Believers

Just before his death in 634
C.E., after consulting the senior
Sahaba, Abu Bakr chose Umar as his
successor by declaring, "My brothers in
faith, I have not appointed any of my own
relatives as your Caliph, but Umar. Do you accept
this decision?" The people responded, "We listen and we obey!"
Umar accepted the position reluctantly.

Following Abu Bakr's death, Umar addressed the people
gathered in Masjid un Nabi.

"…..In the performance of my duties, I will seek guidance from
the Quran and will follow the examples set by Prophet ﷺ and
Abu Bakr. In this task I seek your help. If I follow the right
path, follow me. If I stray from the right path, correct me so

that we are not led astray..." Umar went on to say, "...Read the Quran. Acquire knowledge through it and act upon it. Thus you will become the followers of the Quran. Keep holding yourself to account before you are held to account, for self-examination will render your accounting easy. And weigh yourselves before you are weighed; and prepare yourselves for the great trial when you are produced before Allah Most High. On that day, nothing of your hidden matters will remain covered."

After two visitors to Madinah had referred to Umar as "Ameer ul Mu'mineen" (Leader of the Believers), he decided to use this title, and it was later used by all the Caliphs.

Riches of Persia

In 635 C.E the Muslim army left Madinah for Iraq under the command of Saad bin Abi Waqqas to face the Persians and take back what they had conquered. Umar determined the route and the places where the army would stop. He even studied the maps of the area in making these decisions, drawing upon his experience of previous journeys. He divided the troops into regiments, chose the commanders and gave instructions after carefully considering every detail. In short, he made all the essential decisions. Then Umar asked Saad bin Abi Waqqas to offer peace to the Persians and use diplomacy to avoid a battle. Fourteen Muslim chiefs of different tribes

were sent as envoys. But the peace initiative failed and the battle began in 636 CE. It was a long battle in which the Persians used elephants as 'tanks'. Muslims were victorious in the end, even though their army was much smaller. Rustam, the legendary Persian commander, was also killed during this battle.

Some time later, after taking the White Palace on the banks of the River Tigris in Madain from the Persians, Saad sent enormous treasure to Madinah.

Upon seeing the glittering pile in the Masjid un Nabi, Umar's eyes swelled up with tears.

One of the men present commented, "There is nothing to cry about." Umar responded, "I am crying because riches give rise to hostility and mutual hatred. A nation which has these evils loses

its respect!" Umar praised the honesty of the Muslim soldiers who had not kept back anything unlawfully. "O Ameer ul Mu'mineen, when you yourself set such a high example of honesty, why should your people not be honest?" said Ali.

On To Jerusalem

When Jerusalem was under siege by the Muslim generals in 637 C.E., and the mighty Byzantine army was defeated, the Christians decided to give in. They had heard about the just and tolerant ways of the Muslims in dealing with the people of the conquered places. However, they insisted that the Caliph himself must come and sign the peace treaty, as they wanted to make sure that they would be treated well. Therefore, a letter was sent to the

Caliph explaining their condition and requesting him to come to Palestine.

On receiving this letter, Umar Farooq left Madinah for Jerusalem with only one servant and one camel. As he left the city, he said to his servant, "We are two and the mount is one. If I ride and you go on foot, I shall be doing you an injustice. And if we both ride, that will be an injustice to the camel. So we better take it in turns to ride." So they alternately rode and went on foot, then they would both go on foot for some time to give the camel some respite. They went on in this way until they were approaching Jerusalem, when, by chance, it was the

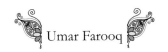

servant's turn to ride. The servant declined to sit on the camel's back so that the Caliph might be on the mount while entering the city. But Umar Farooq did not agree to this. And so the Caliph reached the gates of Jerusalem with the servant on the camel's back and himself on foot wearing rough clothes. The inhabitants gaped at the sight which they could not even have imagined. Witnessing this sight, the priests opened the gates and directly made peace with Umar Farooq.

Umar signed the following agreement; an example of a more just and considerate treaty is difficult to be found in history:

"This is the protection that the servant of Allah, Umar bin Al Khattab, Ameer ul Mu'mineen, has offered to all the people of Jerusalem. The protection is for their lives and properties, their churches and their crosses, their sick and healthy. Their churches shall not be used as homes nor shall they be destroyed. There should be no compulsion on them in the matter of religion. If anyone wishes to leave, they can leave freely and take their belongings." After the completion of the peace treaty, Caliph Umar made a short speech in which he said:

"O people of Palestine, what is for us is for you. What is not for us is not for you either."

The Mosque of Umar

During this visit he went with the Patriarch to visit various holy places. One day when Umar was sitting in the courtyard of the Church of Qiama in Jerusalem, the time came for the afternoon prayer. Umar then turned to the Patriarch and asked where he should say his prayers. The priest replied that he could pray right where he was seated. Umar, however, said, "No, it is not proper for Umar to pray inside the Church, because any Muslim who comes here afterwards, will maintain that since Umar has said his prayers here, a mosque should be built on that very spot." Umar, therefore, moved a stone's throw away, and said his prayers. Muslims did come to the city later on and, as he had foreseen, built their mosque at the exact point where he had said his prayers. This mosque exists to this day – a short, but discreet distance away from the Church. This discretion shown by Umar is all the more remarkable for his having been the ruler of Palestine at that time and, therefore, in a position to do anything he wished. A man with less foresight would have

regarded praying inside the Church as a harmless event. But Umar could foresee that this act could in future become a cause of dispute and unnecessary trouble.

The Great Welfare State

During Umar's Caliphate, Egypt, Iraq, Palestine, Persia and Syria, a total area of 2,251,030 square miles, came under Islamic rule. The conquered territories were dealt with tolerance. Jews and Christians who had been persecuted under the Byzantines appreciated this. Their customs and rules were taken into account while making laws, something hitherto unheard of.

During his Caliphate many new cities were founded like Kufa, Basra and Fustat. These cities were properly planned, and many mosques, orphanages, market places, public utilities and administrative buildings

were constructed. He was against the construction of palatial buildings. Umar stood for simplicity and austerity. Much public work was done all over the empire. Canals were dug to irrigate fields and roads and bridges were constructed for public use. Many shelters, guest houses, wells and eating places were built on the roadsides for the public. Prison houses and military cantonments were made along with stables for the cavalry at various strategic points.

Caliph Umar established a new administrative structure. Departments of the army, police, education, judiciary, public works and public treasury were formed. He was the first ruler in the history of the world to separate judiciary from the executive. The *Qadis* (Judges) were chosen for their integrity and learning in Islamic law. Nowhere had anything like this ever been done before. Umar created laws which showed complete human consideration, such as no army personnel

being sent away from their families for more than four months at a time.

Servants of God

He selected and appointed honest and capable men to high positions with the approval and consent of the *Sahaba*. Umar would also take a promise from them to lead a simple life and told them, "Remember, I have not appointed you as commanders and tyrants over the people. I have sent you as leaders, so that people may follow your example. Do not behave as if you are superior to them, for that would amount to cruelty." The appointed governors and officers were given powers and obligations

in the presence of others in order to keep the public informed of their rights. They were expected to keep their doors open without a security guard.

A written list of an officer's possessions was kept as a record. If any unusual financial increase was reported, the officers would be summoned to give explanations. Any invalid increase would be confiscated and sent to *Bait ul Mal* (public treasury). At the time of *Hajj* all the officers were required to come to Makkah. People from all over the Islamic world had a chance to voice their grievances against any officer and their concerns were taken care of immediately.

Umar would make enquiries about governors from envoys from the lands he ruled over. Was he a ruler who cared about his subjects, did he visit slaves and walk in funeral processions? Was he accessible to his people and sympathetic towards those who came to his door? If the answers were that he heard cases sympathetically and looked after slaves well, Umar would permit

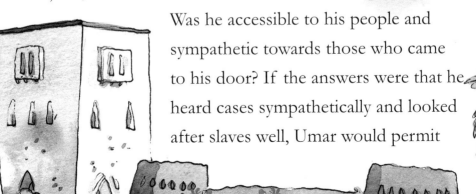

his rule to continue, but otherwise he would promptly appoint another governor to relieve him of his post.

He did not just give orders but saw to it that they were carried out. Whatever Umar expected from the governors he himself did, in fact, he did much more than he asked them to do. Umar not only set an example but also applied stricter rules to himself. His officers were paid a high salary, while what he drew was at poverty level.

Umar had the highest regard for human equality and human respect. This, in effect, removed all kinds of differences between men. Umar even treated Muslims and non-Muslims equally. He was completely just in his dealings as a ruler and also as a person. The following event illustrates this.

The Horse Race

Amr ibn al-As was the governor of Egypt during his Caliphate. One day the governor organized a horse race in which his own son, Muhammad ibn Amr ibn al-As, also took part. But in the race, the horse of the governor's son

was beaten by the horse of a Copt, a non-Muslim. The Copt expressed his joy and this hurt the governor's son. He lashed the Copt with his whip, saying, "Take that! I am the son of a nobleman!"

The Copt came from Egypt to Madinah, the capital, and complained to Umar that the governor's son had whipped him. Umar asked him to stay in Madinah and, after enquiring into the details and discovering the truth, he immediately sent a special messenger to bring Amr ibn al-As and his son without delay to Madinah. When

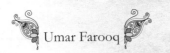

they arrived, they were both brought before the Caliph. Then the latter sent for the young Copt and asked him if this was the man who had beaten him. When the Copt replied in the affirmative, the Caliph handed him a whip and asked him to flog this 'son of a nobleman.' The Copt did so, and went on flogging him till he felt that justice had been done. Then the Caliph asked him also to flog Amr ibn al-As, the father of the young wrongdoer, as it had been his high status – as Umar explained – which had encouraged the son to take his whip to him. But then the Copt said, "No,

I have whipped the person who whipped me, and I wish no more than that."

Umar said to the Copt: 'By God! If you had beaten him (the governor) we would not have intervened, until you yourself had stopped beating him. Then Umar turned

to Amr ibn al-As and said: 'O Amr, since when have you enslaved people who were born free?

A Common Man

Many times when foreign envoys or messengers came to Madinah, they found him resting under a palm tree or in the mosque amongst the people, and it was difficult to distinguish which man was the Caliph.

Caliph Umar Farooq, ruled over a large part of Asia and Africa, but continued to wear very ordinary clothes which often had patches. He would carry water bags over his shoulders. He would sleep on the ground with a stone as a pillow. He ate simple food and lived in an ordinary house.

Some people from Iraq once came to see Umar. When it was time for food, he brought them a big bowl containing whole wheat bread and olive oil, and asked them to eat. They started eating very slowly, and a little at a time. "I can see what you are doing, people of Iraq," Umar said to them. "You know, if I wanted, I could have lavish and delicious food such as you have. But we leave over our portion of the world so that we may

partake of it in the Hereafter. Have you not heard what Allah said about a certain group of people? 'You wasted away your precious things in your earthly life.'"

Once Ahnaf ibn Qays came to see him in Madinah. He found him desperately running around. When Ahnaf asked Umar what was the matter, he replied that a camel belonging to *Bait al-Mal* (public treasury) had gone astray and that he was looking for it. Ahnaf said, "You are the leader of the believers *(Amirul-Muminin)*. Why are you taking all this trouble? You should have asked a servant to do this for you." Caliph Umar replied, "Who is a greater servant than I am?"

Considering oneself a common man, while in actuality being the ruler of an empire, gave a practical example of the humility expected of a ruler who obeyed the Islamic code of ethics.

The Burden of Umar

Caliph Umar often spent nights going around the city to see whether anyone needed help. He used to visit the old and sick and even did their housework. He also visited the families of the soldiers to ensure that they were taken care of.

One night as usual, during
the year of the famine
(640 C.E) Umar went on
his rounds to make sure
no one went to sleep hungry.
He came to a dwelling where he
saw a woman cooking something and
a couple of children sitting nearby and

crying. Umar went up to her to inquire what the matter was. He was told that they had not had any food and to console the children she was pretending to cook. "I am pretending to cook food but it is just water and stones. I am doing this in the hope that they will get exhausted and go to sleep!"

Umar felt accountable, for he thought he had made arrangements to ensure that everyone had sufficient food. He left immediately and went to the *Bait ul Mal* (public treasury) and put the necessary provisions in a bag. Umar asked Aslam, his slave, to load the bag on his back. Aslam offered to carry it for him. The Caliph carried the bag himself saying, "On the Day of Judgment, you will not be there to carry my burden for me."

Discontent

One day, Firoz, a Persian nicknamed 'Abu Lulu' complained to Umar about the taxes he had to

pay. When Umar told him, after twice enquiring into the matter, that the taxes were reasonable, he became very upset. The next day during the *Fajr* prayer, he stabbed the Caliph six times and also wounded thirteen Muslims. He was uncontrollable. At last realizing that he could not escape, he stabbed himself to death. When Umar learned who the assassin was, he said, "Thank Allah he is not a Muslim!"

Umar prayed to Allah to pardon him, "If I had the earth full of gold, then I would give it in order to free myself of the Lord's punishment before it descends on me." Hearing this, someone said to Umar that he had rendered great services to religion. He would surely have a great position with Allah. Umar replied, "If there is nothing for me or against me that will be enough."

The Last Wish of Umar

Umar asked his son Abdullah to go to Ayisha and beg her permission to be buried by the side of the Prophet. Ayisha wept saying, "I wanted to reserve this spot for my own grave, but I prefer Umar to myself!" When Umar heard that she had consented, he sighed with relief, "It was the greatest wish of my life!"

Before he breathed his last, Umar, like a true believer, said to his son, "Rub my cheek in the dust, Abdullah," and his son did as he was asked. Then with his head resting on the ground, Umar uttered these words: "Woe betide you, Umar, and woe betide the one who gave birth to you if Allah does not forgive you." In death also he showed his humility. He had spent his life in the service of Allah and in establishing the ideals of Islam, but he felt as if he had done nothing.

Umar Farooq, one of the greatest Caliph of Islam passed away

on 1ˢᵗ of Muharram 644 C.E. after serving for ten years, six months and four days.

He did not nominate his successor but suggested that he who had the largest number of votes from among the six *Sahaba* (Companions) should be chosen. He advised his successor, whoever it was going to be, to fear Allah and protect the rights of the people (Muslims and non-Muslims) and always to keep his word.

His Caliphate, a great welfare state, was the highest point in early Islamic history. The old, the poor, the orphans and the disabled, both Muslims and non-Muslims alike were provided for from the *Bait ul Mal.* Everyone was equal and was treated with justice. Undoubtedly Umar Farooq was an exemplary human being and an ideal ruler.

Uthman Ibn Affan

(May Allah be pleased with him)

The Third Caliph of Islam
576 C.E. - 656 C.E.

Uthman the Rich

Uthman was born around 576 C.E. in Taaif.

Thus he was about six years younger than the Prophet Muhammad ﷺ. Both his parents, Affan and Urwa, were distant relatives of the Prophet ﷺ, Uthman received a formal education and was one of the few people in Makkah who could read and write.

Affan, a very rich merchant, died when Uthman was just twenty years old. Uthman, who inherited a great deal of wealth at his father's death, followed his father's profession. His straightforwardness combined with his ability to trade soon made him the richest person amongst the Quraish. He came to be known as 'Uthman Ghani' (Uthman the Rich). But he was best known for his modesty and good character. The Prophet Muhammad ﷺ once said, "Uthman is the most modest of my Companions!" Even before accepting Islam, he never gambled or drank wine. He was an honest man and this was reflected in all his business and social dealings. He led a simple life and was regularly engaged in helping others and in doing social work to assist hundreds of widows,

orphans and the poor. He was also helpful and kind towards his relatives. All this testified to his nobility of character.

Uthman was also famous for his handsome looks. In spite of his wealth and good looks, he went out of his way to make sure that his behaviour did not hurt anyone. He was not at all arrogant. On the contrary, he was soft spoken and never tried to impose his views on others. All these qualities made him a popular and well-liked person.

Abu Bakr: A Friend Indeed

Even before he accepted Islam, Uthman had great admiration for the Prophet Muhammad ﷺ and would often seek his advice.

Abu Bakr and Uthman were close friends. They would frequently discuss the purpose of creation. When the Prophet Muhammad ﷺ declared his mission, Uthman called on Abu Bakr. Both men talked about it and Abu Bakr informed his friend that he had already accepted Islam. Abu Bakr then

encouraged his friend to do so too. Both went to see the Prophet ﷺ. Uthman did not hesitate to take the *Shahada* (Article of Faith: "There is no deity but Allah and Muhammad is His servant and Messenger.") From then on he became a very devout Muslim and remained so until his death.

The Quraish reacted violently to Uthman's conversion to Islam. Even his relatives turned against him, but he stood firm in his new faith. The Prophet Muhammad appreciated his sacrifices and gave Uthman his daughter Ruqayyah in marriage.

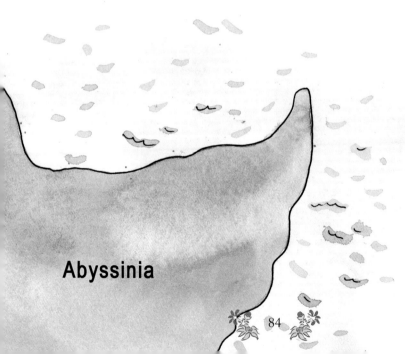

Abyssinia

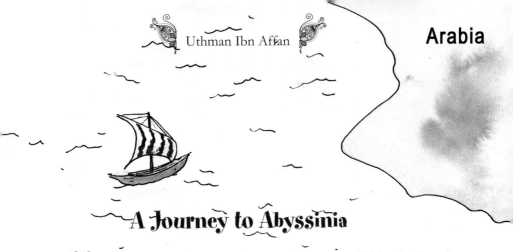

A Journey to Abyssinia

The conditions in Makkah were becoming very difficult for the Muslims. The boycott by the Quraish added to their misery. So Uthman and Ruqayyah asked the Prophet for his permission to leave Makkah for Abyssinia. He acceded to their request, gave them his blessings and prayed for their safety. At the time of their departure he said, "After the Prophet Lut, Uthman is the first to migrate with his family in the way of Allah." Very shortly thereafter, some other Muslims followed them to Abyssinia.

In Abyssinia, Allah blessed Uthman and Ruqayyah with a son, whom they named Abdullah. Two years later, they returned to Makkah, having heard that the conditions for the Muslims had improved. Upon their arrival, they found out that the information they had received was incorrect.

During his stay in Makkah, Uthman spent most of his time in the company of the Prophet Muhammad ﷺ. He freed several slaves and continued to help the poor, especially during the social boycott imposed upon the Muslims by the Quraish.

The Generosity

In 622 C.E, Uthman and Ruqayyah migrated again but this time to Madinah. They number among the very few people who ever had the honour of migrating twice for the sake of Allah. In Madinah, Uthman's business started to flourish and he soon became one of the richest people there as well.

When the Muhajirs first came to Madinah, they had great difficulty in getting drinking water. There was just one well and its owner would not allow Muslims to draw any water unless

they paid a high price for it.
The Prophet Muhammad ﷺ
asked, "Who is there who will
buy this well for the Muslims?
Allah will reward him with a
fountain in Paradise." Uthman
responded immediately. He
bought the well for twenty
thousand dirhams and
donated it to the Muslims.

The Possessor of Two Lights

After the Prophet
Muhammad ﷺ migrated
to Madinah, he visited

Uthman and Ruqayyah frequently and enjoyed playing with his grandson, Abdullah. The couple were content and lead a happy life. Alas, their happiness was short-lived. In 624 C.E. after a brief illness, Ruqayyah passed away. Uthman was grief-stricken.

Realizing that he was no longer a son-in-law of the Prophet made him even sadder. The Prophet Muhammad ﷺ sensed this. About a year later, the Prophet gave his second daughter, Umm Kulthum in marriage to Uthman. He told his daughter that he found a resemblance in Uthman to his forefather Ibrahim.

Thus Uthman earned the title of "Dhun Nurain", which means "the possessor of two lights." He was called this because he was married to two of the Prophet's daughters. Umm Kulthum loved Abdullah and took good care of him.

The Tidings of Paradise

When Masjid un Nabi could not accommodate the growing number of Muslims, the Prophet was obliged to ask, "Who is there to pay for the extension of this Masjid?" Again it was Uthman who stepped forward to take the responsibility.

Whenever help was needed, Uthman never hesitated to donate generously to the cause of Islam. On one occasion, Uthman's contribution was the largest. He gave one thousand camels, fifty horses and one thousand pieces of gold. When the Prophet Muhammad ﷺ saw what Uthman had given, he gave him the tidings of Paradise and said, "Whatever Uthman does from this day on will do him no harm!"

This happy marriage of Uthman and Umm Kulthum did not last long either. Umm Kulthum died six years after her marriage in 630 C.E., without having had any children. Her father led the funeral prayers. Earlier, Abdullah had died at about the age of eight, two years after his own mother's death. Abdullah's funeral prayer was also led by the Prophet ﷺ. Uthman clung to the fond memories of both Ruqayyah and Umm Kulthum for the rest of his life.

For the Cause of Islam

In 639 C. E., during the caliphate of Umar, there was a famine in Arabia that caused the people great hardship. When a caravan brought in a large shipment of grains that belonged to Uthman,

the merchants offered to buy it at double the price, which would have given Uthman a huge profit. They were told that he had already made a deal at a much higher price. The merchants were curious to know who had made such an offer. Uthman informed them that it was Allah. After that, he distributed the entire stock amongst the needy.

Uthman was one of the few people who wrote down *ayat* (verses) of the Quran at the time they were revealed. He had also memorized the whole of the Quran. Even after the death of the Prophet Muhammad ﷺ, Uthman was held in high esteem by the Companions because of his noble nature and closeness to the Holy Prophet. He served as an advisor during the caliphates of Abu Bakr and Umar.

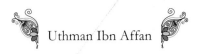

The Next Caliph

While lying on his deathbed, and after much thought, Umar appointed six of the Prophet's most prominent Companions to

elect the next Caliph. To all of them, the Prophet had given the tidings of Paradise.

This committee of six gave Abdul Rahman bin Auf (one of the committee members) the task of selecting the leader. He interviewed several people, including the Bedouin chiefs who were in Madinah to attend Umar's funeral. He analyzed their answers, took into consideration the views of the public and prayed to Allah for guidance before making up his mind.

Abdul Rahman bin Auf selected Uthman Ibn Affan and told him, "Promise that you will act according to the commandments of the Quran and the example set by the Prophet and his two Caliphs." Uthman pledged, "I promise to

do that to the best of my knowledge and ability!" While he was speaking, the awareness of this great responsibility made his body shiver. Thus, at the age of seventy, in 644 C.E, Uthman became the third Caliph of Islam. People reacted favorably to Uthman's election.

The Rope of Allah

After accepting the position, Uthman gave several directives setting guidelines for the heads of various departments and warned them that Allah would cause them to be replaced with others if they abused their authority.

The civil officers were given the following guidelines:

"….Allah requires the administrators to be the well-wishers and protectors of the people. You are not just officers but protectors as well. Learn about people's problems and help in solving them. Ensure that there is a balance between the duties and the rights of the people…..whatever promises are made, even to enemies, should be respected."

The officers of the military were told, "You are to protect the life and property of both Muslims and non-Muslims.

The laws made hitherto under Umar were made as a result of consultations, therefore do not breach them."

The tax collectors were advised, "Allah enjoins justice, therefore, be just and fair to all. Be honest and pay particular attention to the orphans and the poor. See that the people are not taxed beyond their capacity. Do not oppress or harass the people."

And the general public was also reminded, "Follow Islam faithfully and do not introduce any *bid'ah* (innovations).

Remain united, make sure
that unity is maintained at
all costs and hold on tightly to the
'Rope of Allah'." In another sermon he
encouraged people to do as many good deeds
as possible before death knocked on their doors.

The Standard Quran

In 650 C.E., concerns were raised about the recitation of
the Quran. The Iraqis recited it in one way and the Syrians
in another way. The people of Kufa were reciting it in yet
another way. This was causing a dispute. As usual, Uthman
brought the matter before the senior Companions for
consultation. They agreed that a standardized text of the

Quran had to be prepared to avoid further disputes that might cause division amongst the people. A committee was formed and entrusted with this sacred task. So he had the distinction of uniting the Muslim community on a uniform version of the Quran.

During the Caliphate of Abu Bakr, the Quran had been compiled under strict guidelines in the form of a book. This original copy was first kept in the custody of Ayesha and later on in that of Hafsa, both wives of the Prophet Muhammad ﷺ

The committee members were: Zaid bin Thabit, (one of the original main scribes during the Prophet's lifetime), Abdullah bin Zubair, Saeed bin Al 'As and Abdur Rahman bin Auf.

Occasionally, Uthman had also performed this task as well. After the committee

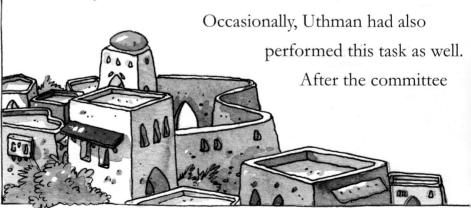

had completed its task, they read out this version to the gatherings of Muhajirs and Ansars three times. It was also compared with the original copy and no discrepancies were found. Uthman, being a 'Hafiz' himself, double checked for accuracy and approved it. Copies of this edition were prepared and distributed to all the provinces. Thus, Uthman had the honour of preserving the original Quran that has remained intact to this day!

Concern for the Ummah

It was Uthman who started the tradition of supplying free meals to everyone during Ramadan at *Iftaar* (breaking of fast) time. The *mu'azzins* (those who called the people to prayers) started receiving salaries. For the convenience of the people, the second call, was introduced for Friday prayers.

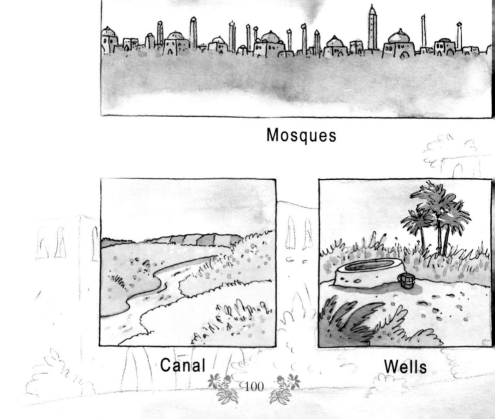

Mosques

Canal

Wells

Uthman was very active in building projects and doing things to improve the daily lives of the *Ummah* (community). Uthman was the first Caliph to have the Masjid un Nabi and the Grand Masjid in Makkah extended and beautified. As many as five thousand mosques were also built and arrangements were made for their upkeep. Hundreds of canals and wells were dug to increase the water supply and to develop agriculture. Guesthouses were

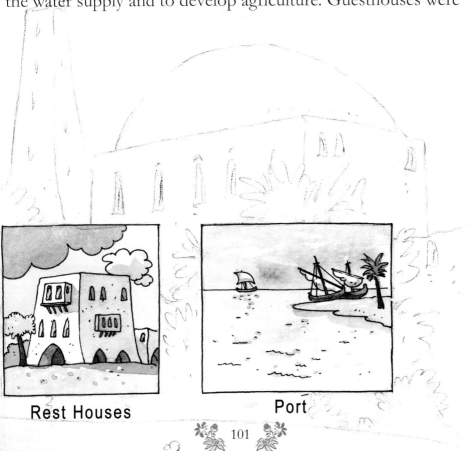

Rest Houses   **Port**

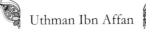
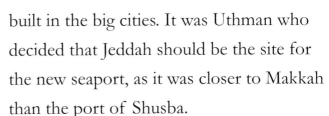

built in the big cities. It was Uthman who decided that Jeddah should be the site for the new seaport, as it was closer to Makkah than the port of Shusba.

The Spread of Islam

A naval force was established for the first time after Uthman reluctantly gave permission to face the Roman navy that attacked the Muslims at every opportunity. Eventually, under Ameer Muawiyah and Abdullah bin Sarah, the Muslim navy became a powerful force to reckon with and remained so for several centuries. During his caliphate, Islamic rule was consolidated in Persia and Egypt and spread to the whole of North Africa and also across some parts of Spain. It even spread to Azerbaijan, Armenia, Kabul and Ghazni.

The economic policies of Uthman brought prosperity to the people. Some very quickly became rich and this became a source of resentment for others. Contrary to the Islamic teaching of brotherhood, some of the Quraish started developing a sense of superiority, thus weakening the bond of unity.

False Rumours

By the middle of Uthman's caliphate, most of the senior companions had passed away and the faith of the younger generation was not as strong as that of the previous one. Islam had enjoined obedience to its leaders but there were some who even started questioning the authority of the Caliph, while others spread wrong information about him. Uthman did not take a salary from the state. He supported his needy relatives and kinsmen financially by drawing upon his own wealth. Yet, people quite erroneously believed that he helped his relatives and kinsmen by dipping into the funds of the *Bait ul Mal* (Public Treasury).

Uthman had continued the policy of Umar, by not distributing the conquered lands amongst the soldiers. The previous owners had the right to keep their own property. The army demanded that Uthman should change this policy. Discontent quietly spread when he did not give in to the army's demand. Later on, the unhappy soldiers indirectly supported the rebels.

The Peaceful Option

Umar had ruled with a firm hand, but people took advantage of Uthman, who was very mild-natured and kind-hearted, often overlooking

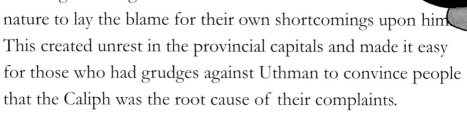

the faults of others. It was
the officers, governors,
and people whom
he loved and trusted
the most who took
advantage of his good
nature to lay the blame for their own shortcomings upon him. This created unrest in the provincial capitals and made it easy for those who had grudges against Uthman to convince people that the Caliph was the root cause of their complaints.

Uthman did his best to control the situation and satisfy the dissenters. He addressed the people in the Masjid un Nabi, patiently explaining his position in detail about the allegations made against him. He called meetings with some senior Companions, including Ali ibn Abi Talib, for consultations. Although he was advised to use force against the rebels, Uthman declined that option. He felt that it was against the teachings of Islam to shed the blood of a Muslim.

Opposition to the Caliph gained momentum and was becoming dangerous. He was determined not to use force at any cost and was prepared to risk his own life to avoid division and bloodshed amongst the Muslims. He had heard the Prophet

Muhammad ﷺ say that there would be no end to a civil war once it started. Uthman did not want to be the one to start it off.

The Last Sermon

The last sermon of Uthman was highly significant. He said:

"The truth is that you are in this world merely to prepare for the next world. Allah never intended that you should be attracted by the world. This world will not last; the hereafter alone will be eternal. Therefore, you should not be proud of anything in this world. Beware that you do not become forgetful of the next world. Prefer the hereafter to this world, for you have ultimately to return to Allah. Always fear Allah….."

In the month of Shawwal, 35 Hijrah (656 C.E)

three armed groups of rebels came to Madinah from Egypt, Kufa and Basra. They studied the situation in Madinah and, when they realized that there would be no resistance, they surrounded the Caliph's house.

Uthman was not allowed to leave the house to go to the Masjid un Nabi for prayers. Even food and water were withheld. The siege continued for 40 days. Uthman was convinced that his time for martyrdom had arrived as predicted by his beloved Prophet ﷺ. Hence he made some preparations. It was Friday, 18th Zilhijjah and he decided to fast, freed twenty slaves, put on new clothes and started reciting the Quran.

Hasan, Husain, grandsons of the Prophet Muhammad ﷺ, Abdullah bin Zubair and other youths were guarding the front of the Caliph's house. Some rebels forced their way through the back and brutally assassinated the 82-year old third Caliph.

May God Be Pleased With Him

Uthman was an extremely religious man who would spend his nights praying. At night, he used to fetch the water for the *wudu* himself instead of waking up his servants, as he believed that they deserved their rest. He liberated a slave every Friday.

Uthman was kind, peace-loving and tolerant. He followed Islam strictly and his love for the Prophet Muhammad ﷺ had no bounds. He was one of the first to memorize the Quran from cover to cover. He regarded the responsibility of the caliphate as a sacred duty and believed that he was answerable to Allah. No wonder the Prophet Muhammad ﷺ had given him the glad tidings of Paradise not once but three times. Therefore, it may be said that rebellion against Uthman was a rebellion against Islam. May Allah be pleased with him, ameen.

Ali
Ibn Abi Talib
(May Allah be pleased with him)

The Fourth Caliph of Islam
600 C.E. - 661 C.E.

The Clan of Banu Hashim

Before the days of Islam the Arabs grouped themselves in tribes, clans and families. The Quraysh were a powerful merchant tribe that controlled Makkah and also its Kabah when the religion of Islam was founded. At the time of the Prophet Muhammad's birth, the Quraysh ruled Makkah.

The Banu Hashim was an important branch of the powerful Quraysh tribe. It takes its name from Hashim, the great-grandfather of the Prophet Muhammad ﷺ.

Abdul Muttalib belonged to the clan of Banu Hashim. He was the Prophet's grandfather. He had ten sons; noteworthy among them were Abdullah, Hamza, Abbas, Abu Talib, and Abu Lahab. The house of Abdul Muttalib of Banu Hashim of Quraysh comprised a form of nobility in pre-Islamic Makkah, based upon their duty to act as stewards and caretakers of the pilgrims coming to Makkah to worship at the Kabah. This duty had been handed down to them from generation to generation.

The Prophet's father, Abdullah, died before his birth; his mother, Amina, died some seven years later. After

the death of his mother, the Prophet's grandfather took care of him. But two years later Abdul Muttalib also passed away in around 578 A.D.

Abu Talib

The protection of the Prophet now fell to Abu Talib, his

uncle. Despite his poverty, Abu Talib was the noblest and the most hospitable and, therefore, the most respected among the Quraysh. No wonder that the protection of young Muhammad ﷺ was left to him.

Ali was born to Abu Talib in 600 A.D., ten years before the Prophet received his first revelation. Ali's mother was Fatimah bint Asad. The Prophet regarded Fatimah as her own mother and held her in high regard.

Apart from Ali, who was the youngest of all, Abu Talib had three sons and two daughters from his wife Fatimah bint Asad– Talib, Aqil, Jafar, Umm Hani and Jumanah.

The Prophet Takes Ali into His Care

Following his marriage to Khadijah, the Prophet moved out of his uncle's house and began to live with Khadijah. Khadijah was a tradeswoman of honour and great wealth. Aided by this marriage which provided amply for his needs, Muhammad ﷺ spent his days respected and loved by all the people of Makkah.

Ali's stay with the Prophet dated from a time when poverty was widespread in Makkah. Since Abu Talib had a very large family, the Prophet approached his uncle Abbas, who was the richest member of the Banu Hashim clan, saying, "Your brother Abu Talib has a very large family, and he is in a state of want as a result of this widespread poverty. Let us together lighten his burden and take into our homes some of his children." Abbas agreed and took into his care Jafar, and the Prophet took Ali. Besides their own daughters, Ali, who was still a boy of five years, lived with the Prophet and Khadijah in the same house.

Ali Embraces Islam

Ali, the son of Abu Talib and cousin of the Prophet, came into the Prophet's house while he and Khadijah were praying.

He asked his cousin what they were doing. The Prophet told him that this was Allah's religion, the path that Allah had chosen Himself. It was to call people to this path that He had sent His prophets to the world. "Believe in One Allah," the Prophet said, "He has no partner. Worship Him alone. Forsake the idols Lat and Uzza." "I have heard nothing of this nature before today," Ali replied. "I cannot make a decision until I have talked the matter over with my father, Abu Talib." But the Prophet did not want anyone to know about his secret until the time had come for it to be made public. "Ali," he said. "If you are not ready to become a Muslim, keep the matter to yourself." Ali waited for one night, then Allah turned his heart towards Islam. He went back to the Prophet early in the morning. "What was it that you were telling me yesterday?" he asked. "Bear witness that there is none worthy of being served save Allah. He is One. He has no partner. Forsake Lat and Uzza, and disown all those who are set up as equals with Allah." Ali did this and became a Muslim. Then, in fear of Abu Talib, he used to come and see the Prophet secretly. Ali kept his Islam a secret; he did not tell anyone about it." Ali was then the first youth to enter Islam.

An Invitation to Accept the Faith

When the Prophet felt it his duty to preach in public, he became very conscious of the greatness of this task, realizing that it would require his undivided attention. He hoped that his family would look after him financially so that, freed from having to look for a livelihood; he would be able to concentrate on his preaching work. He called Abdul Muttalib's family together in his own house. There were about thirty family members at the time. The Prophet told them what his true mission in life now was. He asked for their support, so that he would be free to discharge his prophetic duties.

"Banu Abdul Muttalib," the Prophet said, "I have been sent to you in particular, and to the whole of mankind in general. Who will swear allegiance to me and become my brother and companion? Who will fulfill my debts and my promises on my behalf? Who will look after my family affairs for me? He will be with me in heaven."

The Prophet's own family was not ready to accept responsibility for him. Abbas ibn Abdul Muttalib, the Prophet's uncle, was rich enough to look after his nephew. Yet even he remained silent, for fear that this responsibility would devour his wealth. Only Ali, who was a child of about twelve years, stood up and said, "I take your responsibility, O messenger of Allah!" On hearing Ali's response, the Prophet said, "You, O Ali, you O Ali!" None of the elders was ready to help the Prophet. Allah, however, helped His Prophet, first through the Prophet's wife, Khadijah bint Khuwaylid, and later on through Abu Bakr, whose wealth saw the Prophet through the years in Madinah.

Makkan Opposition

Some people were only familiar with religion in a particular, set form. To them, the message of Islam just appeared to put their elders in the wrong. Abu Jahl declared: "He thinks we are all fools, and considers our ancestors woefully astray. He insults our idols." "He is insane, without doubt," Umayyah added.

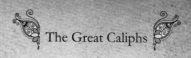

For some people it was the threat of financial loss, which prevented them from accepting the message of Islam. The House of Allah at Makkah had been turned into a house of idol worship before the coming of the Prophet. People of every religion had placed their idols there. This was why four months had been made sacred — so that people would be free to visit the Kabah. During the four months that people used to flock to Makkah, Makkan traders did very good business. Were the idols to be removed

from the Kabah, people would stop visiting the city, and its inhabitants would suffer immense losses. So there were many people with a stake in keeping up polytheistic practices. Thus the Quraysh became opposed to the Prophet's mission of monotheism.

The Demands of the Quraysh

The Quraysh once presented a demand to the chief of the Banu Hashim, the Prophet's uncle, Abu Talib, that he should expel his nephew from the tribe. Only then would they be able to slay the Prophet. Abu Talib's honour prevented him from taking this step. When Abu Talib, at the Quraysh's behest, asked

his nephew to stop criticizing their gods, the Prophet became concerned that his uncle was going to hand him over to the Quraysh. For just one moment Abu Talib hesitated between the enmity of his people and the cause of his nephew. Immediately, he called the Prophet back. "Go forth, my nephew," he said, "and say what you will. By the same Allah I swear I shall never betray you to your enemies."

Three Years Ban

The Quraysh decided that they and all others would have nothing to do with the whole of the Banu Hashim family. A ban stopped inter-marriage and commercial relations. As a result of this boycott, the whole of the Banu Hashim clan, with the exception of Abu Lahab, were forced to live apart in a mountain ravine, called Shi'b Abi Talib.

The manner in which these people quietly endured all this cruel oppression was bound to have an effect on the conscience of others. And it did. Within three years, people like Abul Bakhtari, Hisham ibn Amr, Zubayr ibn Umayyah, Zamah ibn al-Aswad and Mut'im ibn Adi broke away from the ranks of the enemy, openly challenging this wrongful pact by which a boycott had

been imposed on the Banu Hashim. The pact collapsed, and the Banu Hashim were rescued from their terrible plight.

Patience enables us to refrain from taking action, and permits things to take their natural course. Deep down, people always have a soft spot for one who bears abuse quietly, for one who refuses to be provoked even in face of the utmost provocation. The human conscience naturally tends to favour the oppressed rather than the oppressor. When the oppressed stand firm in the face of persecution, they prove themselves to be in the right. The boycott that was imposed on the Prophet and his family in the seventh year of the prophetic mission was just such an example.

Abu Talib Passes Away

Abu Talib became very frail due to the hardships he had to suffer during the three-year boycott. Very soon, after the boycott was lifted, he died. This was the ninth year of prophethood. At the time Ali was nineteen years old.

The tribal system prevalent in the time of the Prophet was one, which gave protection to individuals. It was seldom that anyone could survive without it. After Abu Talib's death, his responsibilities descended upon Abu Lahab. Since Abu Lahab refused to extend any protection to him, the Prophet began seeking the protection of some other tribe, so that he could continue his preaching work. Eventually Mut'im ibn Adi agreed to protect the Prophet, who, shielded by the swords of Mut'im's sons, once again entered the city walls.

On the Night of Hijrah

The people of Makkah did whatever they could to thwart the Prophet and he was subjected to torment upon torment. Together with the Prophet, other Muslims were also persecuted in Makkah. But his mission continued to attract more and more people, and finally the message of Islam reached the people of Madinah, the majority of whom accepted Islam and agreed to give aid to the Muslims. Thus, one by one, the Muslims started emigrating to Madinah.

Finally in 622 A.D. came the Prophet's turn. The Quraysh realized this and contrived to kill the Prophet. However, the Prophet knew exactly what was going on. Quietly, he continued his preparations. On the night of the Hijrah, the Prophet

confided his plan to Ali and asked him to cover himself with his green mantle from Hadramawt and to sleep in his bed. He further asked him to tarry in Makkah until he had returned all things left with the Prophet to their rightful owners. Just before dawn, the Prophet left without being noticed.

When Ali reached Madinah the Prophet was staying at the house of Kulthum ibn Hadm. Ali went to Prophet's house to meet him. There he met the Helpers (Ansar) and other Immigrants (Muhajirin). Not only did the Ansar accommodate the emigrants in their homes; they treated them as brothers and sisters, and shared their possessions with them. And they did all this, fully conscious of the fact that their action involved much more than economic sacrifice. They knew full well that what they were doing would arouse the hostility of the most powerful factions in both Arabia and Persia. There are no words more fitting than those of Ali to describe them: "They were true to their word, steadfast in adversity."

Fatimah and Ali

In the second year of Hijrah the Prophet married his youngest daughter Fatimah to Ali. Then, Fatimah was about eighteen years old and Ali was twenty-two. At the time of their marriage, the Prophet said to Fatimah: "I have married you to the dearest of my family to me."

Ali narrates that when he gave the proposal of marriage, the Prophet asked him, "Do you have something to give in dower (bridal gift)?" Ali confessed that he did not. The

Prophet then asked, "Where is the coat of mail I gave you on so and so occasion?" Ali replied, "I have that." The Prophet said, "Give it in dower of Fatimah." Ali sold this coat for 480 dirhams and gave the dower.

The marriage produced three boys, Hasan, Hussain, and Muhsin (who died in his infancy) and two girls, Zainab and Umm Kulthum.

Jumai ibn Umayr once asked Ayishah whom the Prophet loved most. "Fatimah," she replied. But the Prophet's whole life was moulded by thoughts of the hereafter. He loved his children, but not in any worldly way.

Ali ibn Abi Talib, Fatimah's husband, once told Ibn Abdul Wahid a story about the Prophet's most beloved daughter. Fatimah's hands, he said, were blistered from constant grinding; her neck had become sore from carrying water; her clothes would become dirty from sweeping the floor. When the Prophet had received an influx of servants from some place, Ali suggested to his wife that she approach her father and ask for a servant. She went, but could not speak to the Prophet because of the crowd. Next day, he came to their house, and asked Fatimah why she had wanted to see him. Ali told the Prophet the whole story, and said that he had sent her. "Fear Allah, Fatimah," the Prophet said, "Fulfill your obligations to the Lord, and continue with your housework. And when you go to bed at night, praise Allah thirty-three times, and glorify Him the same number of times; exalt His name thirty-four times, and that will make a full hundred. This would be much better than having a servant." "If that is the will of Allah and His Prophet," Fatimah replied, "then so be it." This was the Prophet's only reply. He did not give her a servant.

Fatimah died six months after the Prophet's death. She was twenty-seven years old at the time of her death.

Treaty of Hudaybiyyah

The Prophet, in obedience to Allah's will, set out for Makkah in the year 6 A.H. along with 1,400 companions. He made it absolutely clear that the Muslims had no intention of fighting anybody, and were just going for Umrah. As expected, the Quraysh advanced to prevent

the Muslims from entering Makkah. The two parties met at Hudaybiyyah, some eleven kilometres from Makkah. Anxious to avoid fighting, the Prophet set up camp then and there. He then sent a message to the Quraysh, suggesting a peace treaty between the two sides. The Quraysh showed how narrowminded they were while the treaty was being compiled. The Prophet dictated to Ali: "This is a peace treaty, which Muhammad, the Messenger of Allah, has agreed upon with Suhail ibn Amr." Suhail objected saying, "Had we considered you the Messenger of Allah, we would not have turned you away from the House of Allah, nor fought with you. You should write 'Muhammad ibn Abdullah.'" The Prophet promptly asked Ali to rub out what he had written. "By Allah,

I cannot do it," replied Ali. The Prophet erased the words himself and dictated, 'Muhammad, the son of Abdullah.' Many of the clauses were more than the Companions could bear. The Muslims felt badly about the treaty.

But this truce, the terms of which appeared so against the Muslims, later brought them huge benefits.

Because of the peace which followed the Muslims gained more from the Treaty of Hudaybiyyah than from any of their campaigns. The Prophet returned to Makkah two years later with 10,000 men, whereas previously the Muslims had numbered no more than 3,000. The great lesson of

Hudaybiyyah is that one should avoid impatience and should not judge matters by appearances alone. The Treaty of Hudaybiyyah which seemed so against the Muslims held great opportunities for them, which only people of insight could see.

The Wealth of True Faith

Missionary activity was such an important part of the Prophet's life, that if one were to put his whole struggle under one heading, this would surely be the one. He did not concentrate on political, economic and social issues, as leaders usually do, but rather devoted his entire time and energy to preaching the word of Allah.

The Prophet Muhammad ﷺ taught his companions to adopt the same attitude. It was not to be their aim to conquer territory or heap up spoils of war. Rather they were to become a source of wealth—the wealth of true faith—for others. When the Prophet entrusted Ali with the Muslim flag in the field of Khaybar, he told his cousin to proceed softly: "And when you reach their fields, call

them to Islam and tell them what their responsibilities to Allah are. By Allah, if the Lord guides just one of them through you to Islam, then that will be better for you than anything upon which the sun rises."

Ali's Profound Knowledge of Islam

Ali resolved matters connected with religion and gave judgment in legal issues. This he did at a time when he was not very aged. At that time there were only a few people who knew how to read and write. Ali had learnt reading and writing from his very childhood. One of Ali's important tasks became to write letters to the people on behalf of the Prophet.

His speeches, sayings and letters were collected in *Nahjul Balaghah*. He was well known among the companions for his deep knowledge and understanding of the Shariah and for his ability in passing judgment on various religious matters. It was Ali who instructed Abul Aswad Duwali to frame the principles of Arabic grammar.

When Abu Bakr became caliph, he consulted Ali in important

matters. Whenever he was faced with difficult problems, he called upon Ali and said: "O Abul Hasan, show us a way out of this,"

After Abu Bakr, Umar became the second caliph. Ali provided the greatest support to him and helped him as a trusted advisor. There were times when Umar faced complicated issues, he would say: "We are faced with a complicated issue, but Abul Hasan is not here."

Ali was one of the electoral council, which was appointed by Umar to choose the third caliph. Finally, Uthman was selected the caliph. After Uthman's death, all the people pledged themselves to Ali ibn Abi Talib, and he therefore, became the Fourth Caliph of Islam.

A Unique Justice

Ali at one time had a coat of armour, which he lost. One day he went to the market in Kufa, where he found that a Jew was selling a coat of armour. On closer inspection, it turned out to be the same coat of armour which he had lost.

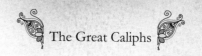

Ali was at that time ruler of the Muslim empire. If he had so desired, he could have taken possession of that coat of armour right there and then. But he did not consider himself above the law, and merely said to the person concerned that the coat of armour belonged to him and then asked him to come to the Qazi (judge), who would decide between them. At that time Shuraih was the Qazi for Muslims. So both of them went to him.

Shuraih in the capacity of Qazi addressed Ali, "O leader of

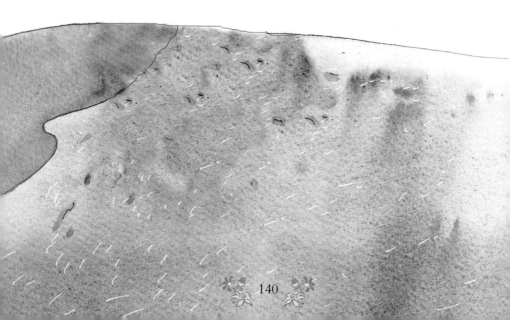

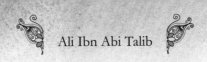
the believers, what you have to say? Ali replied, "This coat of armour is mine. So this should be returned to me." Shuraih then asked the Jew what he had to say. He said that the leader of the believers was not telling the truth for the coat of armour was his. Qazi Shuraih then said to Ali, "I cannot order the coat of armour to be given to you just because of your claim. You must fetch two witnesses in support of your claim."

Ali said that Qazi Shuraih's demand was proper. Then he presented two witnesses, one his slave Qambar and the other, his son, Hasan. Qazi Shuraih said that he would accept the testimony of Qambar, but that he would not accept that of Hasan. Ali asked, 'How is it that you will not accept Hasan as a witness, although according to a *hadith* the Prophet said, "Hasan and Husain are the leaders of the youths of paradise."' Qazi Shuraih said: "That is a different thing. In worldly matters the principle of Islam is that evidence given by children in favour of their fathers is not reliable."

Ali being the Caliph had the power to dismiss the Qazi. But he surrendered before the judgement of the Qazi and withdrew his demand with regard to the coat of armour. On seeing

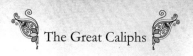

this, the Jew was astonished. He exclaimed: "I bear witness it is by Allah's commandments that the leader of the believers comes to the court like a common man and the Qazi may give a verdict against him. I bear witness that there is none worthy of worship save Him and that Muhammad is the messenger of Allah." Then he said that the coat of armour really belonged to Ali and that once, when it had fallen off Ali's camel, he had

picked it up. Having heard his admission, Ali gave the coat of armour back to him and also gave him seven hundred dirhams.

This story illustrates the principle that the ruler and the ruled are equal in the eyes of the law. In a court of law both must appear on an equal footing and the legal verdict must be equally binding on both of them.

The Simple Life of Ali

Ali lived a very simple life. The many instances of his plain living, strict carrying out of religious duties, and lack of interest in worldly goods are all in record. He would always do his work with his own hands; he would not permit anyone to carry his bags for him. Even if someone went on insisting, he would not agree. If he went to buy clothes with a servant, he would first let the servant choose a garment for himself. Ali would then choose one for himself from the remaining garments.

One day, some one suggested that his clothes were not suitable for the post of a caliph. Ali's reply to this was: "A Caliph does not rule with his clothes, he rules with the responsibility

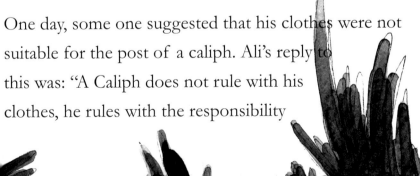

and sense of duty he feels towards Allah." "For," he explained, "these humble clothes protect me from arrogance and haughtiness."

Ali's Death

It was Friday, the seventeenth day of the month of Ramadan, 40 A.H., Ali left for the mosque for the morning prayer. It was still dark. Ibn Muljim also followed him. He quickly drew his poisonous sword and struck Ali from behind. Ali was severely wounded and finally died of the injury a few days later.